鲜香惹味
广东菜

梁燕 编著

做饭

Rice Recipes

广东省出版集团
广东科技出版社
·广州·

图书在版编目（CIP）数据

做饭 / 梁燕编著 .—广州：广东科技出版社，2012.8
（鲜香惹味广东菜）
ISBN 978-7-5359-5715-3

Ⅰ.①做… Ⅱ.①梁… Ⅲ.①粤菜—主食—食谱
Ⅳ.① TS972.13

中国版本图书馆 CIP 数据核字（2012）第 131224 号

本书中文简体版由香港万里机构出版有限公司授权广东科技出版社在中国内地出版发行。
广东省版权局著作权合同登记
图字：19-2012-044 号

责任编辑：赵雅雅　刘　耕　姚　芸
责任校对：黄慧怡
责任印制：罗华之　何小红
出版发行：广东科技出版社
　　　　（广州市环市东路水荫路 11 号　邮政编码：510075）
E-mail：gdkjzbb@21cn.com
http：//www.gdstp.com.cn
经　销：广东新华发行集团股份有限公司
印　刷：东莞市翔盈印务有限公司
　　　　（东莞市东城区莞龙路柏洲边路段　邮政编码：523113）
规　格：889 mm×1 194 mm　1/32　印张 3　字数 70 千
版　次：2012 年 8 月第 1 版
　　　　2012 年 8 月第 1 次印刷
定　价：12.00 元

如发现因印装质量问题影响阅读，请与承印厂联系调换。

忙人、懒人、达人的健康美食攻略

面对大都市快节奏、高压力的生活现状，我们推出了这套《鲜香惹味广东菜》，以**省时、省事、省心、好味、营养**为特色，倡导简约、时尚、健康的饮食理念。书中囊括了广东菜最常见的蒸、炒、煲、炆、煮、炖等烹饪方法，以一日三餐的居家菜为主，强调以味为先，清而不淡，浓而不腻，注重时令，健康为尚。

书中所选食谱均为简单易学，又精致地道的广东特色菜。除了有材料、调料和做法的详细介绍，还包括食材的选购和基本处理方法、常用技巧等技术要点；同时提供每款菜的烹饪时间、人数参考等信息。中英文对照的呈现形式，给即将到国外留学、远离家乡的朋友们提供了不错的参考。"美食达人心动试味"及"Tips"栏目的居家烹饪心得，细致、周到又贴心。

《鲜香惹味广东菜》为都市里的**忙人、懒人、达人**精心设计了一套全面的健康美食攻略，解决您舌尖上的种种疑问，达成您舌尖上的美好愿望。

目录 Contents

看图买材料 Buy ingredients according to the pictures　　　　　1
买回来的材料怎样处理？What to do with the ingredients?　　　5
做饭小贴士 Cooking Tips　　　　　　　　　　　　　　　　　6
煮饭的技巧 Cooking Techniques　　　　　　　　　　　　　　7
一餐中各种食物的摄取比例 The proportion of different food intake during a meal　8
看颜色食果蔬 Choose vegetables and fruit according to colour　　9

开始做饭 Let's Start!

蒸饭 Steamed Rice

海鲜荷叶饭 Seafood rice in lotus leaf　　　　　　　　　　　11
上海菜饭 Shanghai vegetable rice　　　　　　　　　　　　13
番薯饭 Sweet potatoes rice　　　　　　　　　　　　　　　15
杂菌十谷炊饭 Mixed mushrooms rice　　　　　　　　　　　17
豉油鸡糙米饭 Brown rice with soy sauce chicken　　　　　　19
咸鱼肉饼饭 Steamed minced pork with salted fish rice　　　　21
腊肠蒸鸡饭 Steamed chicken rice with preserved sausages　　23
冬菇滑鸡片饭 Steamed chicken and black mushrooms rice　　25
三色有味饭 Trio tasty rice　　　　　　　　　　　　　　　27
海南鸡饭 Hainanese chicken rice　　　　　　　　　　　　29
豉汁排骨凤爪饭 Steamed rice with spareribs, chicken feet and fermented black beans sauce　31

炒饭 Fried Rice

西炒饭 Western fried rice　　　　　　　　　　　　　　　33
扬州炒饭 Yangzhou fried rice　　　　　　　　　　　　　　35
有钱佬炒饭 Richman's fried rice　　　　　　　　　　　　　37
咸鱼鸡粒饭 Fried rice with diced chicken and salted fish　　　39
生炒牛肉饭 Fried rice with beef　　　　　　　　　　　　　41
生炒糯米饭 Stir-fried glutinous rice　　　　　　　　　　　43
肉松姜粒蛋白炒饭 Fried rice with pork floss diced, ginger and egg white　45

菠萝炒饭 Pineapple fried rice	47
鸳鸯炒饭 Duo-colour fried rice	49
福建炒饭 Fujian fried rice	51
红咖喱海鲜炒饭 Fried rice with red curry seafood	53
日式海鲜炒饭 Japanese seafood fried rice	55
牛仔骨咖喱炒饭 Fried rice with curry beef short ribs	57

🍚 其他 Other

台式卤肉饭 Taiwanese pork rice	59
焗猪扒饭 Baked pork chop rice	61
柱侯炆牛腩饭 Rice with stewed spicy beef brisket	63
蚬肉拌饭 Clams rice	65
韩式石头锅饭 Korean stone rice	67
葡国鸡焗饭 Baked portuguese chicken rice	69
番茄盅杂菌饭 Tomato pot with assorted mushrooms rice	71
迷你糯米鸡 Mini steamed glutinous rice with chicken	73
烧鸭泡饭 Rice with roasted duck in soup	75
杂锦冬瓜粒泡饭 Rice with mixed white gourd in soup	77
香芒糯米饭 Glutinous rice with mangoes	79
粢饭 Chinese glutinous rice roll	81
杂菌锅巴 Crispy rice with assorted mushrooms	83

烹饪小词典 Cooking key words

做菜和味道的常用语 Common phrases of cooking and tastes	86
常用调味品（附广东话发音）Common seasonings	87
常用技巧 Common skills	91

看图买材料
Buy ingredients according to the pictures

白米：白米要完整，不要碎，陈米有白点的不要购买。
White rice: completed, not broken. Do not buy old rice with white spot.

珍珠米：大粒，圆润，色白。
Pearl rice: big, round, white.

糙米：完整，带黄色或浅啡色。
Brown rice: completed, slightly yellow or light brown.

红米：颜色比较红，不要暗哑。
Red rice: pretty red, not dim.

1

菠萝：要有香味，但不要有酒味。
Pineapple: smell good without wine aroma.

生菜：颜色翠绿，变黑的不要购买。
Lettuce: green, should not buy if in dim / dark colour.

冬瓜：肉质要结实，不要松。
White gourd: firm texture, not loosen / slacken.

番茄：红色圆润，表示多肉多汁。
Tomato: red, round with juice.

番薯：胭脂红色的番薯比较香。
Sweet potato: pretty red sweet potato gives better smell / aroma.

洋葱：完整，没有花痕或凹痕。
Onion: completed, do not have poor concave mark / stain.

虾米：干身，没有湿气。
Dried shrimp: dry without moisture.

瑶柱：颜色金黄。
Dried scallop: colour is golden brown.

腊肉：色泽要鲜，不要暗哑。
Preserved pork: colour is sharp / bright, not dim.

冬菇：有香味，干身厚肉。
Black mushroom: dry, thick, with good smell / aroma.

烧鸭：要有油光，不干身。
Roasted duck: greasy, not dry.

蚬：蚬壳开了，表示蚬已死，不可买。
Clam: do not buy any clam with open shell.

牛仔骨：颜色要红，不要淤黑。
Beef short rib: colour is pretty red, not dim.

鸡蛋：啡色的鸡蛋比白色的味道更佳。
Egg: brown egg has better taste than white egg.

买回来的材料怎样处理？
What to do with the ingredients?

米 Rice

米放在米缸内，加数粒蒜头可延长储存期。

Put in rice container with several cloves of garlic to keep it longer.

腊味 Preserved pork

煮腊味前先用热水洗去表面的尘和油分。

Wash with hot water to remove dust and oil before cooking.

蚬 Clam

用水养1小时，令蚬吐出沙泥。

Soak in water for 1 hour to remove sand and mud.

菌类 Fungus

要飞水才可去除霉味。
Blanch to get rid of poor / musty smell.

做饭小贴士
Cooking Tips

洋葱 Onion	切洋葱前先将洋葱浸在水中，才不会刺激眼睛。 Soak onion in water before cutting to avoid eye irritation.
炒饭 Shallow-fried rice	要用隔夜的饭，因刚煮熟的饭黏性比较强，炒时会黏在一起。 Use overnight rice as just-cooked rice is more viscous and easily sticking together during shallow frying.
汤饭 Soup rice	不要将汤加入饭来煮，只要将饭放在碗中，然后将汤倒入饭内即可。 Do not cook rice with soup direct. Put rice in bowl and add in soup.
糙米 Brown rice	颗粒较硬，要比平时煮饭的水多加1/3，饭才会适口。 Brown grain is pretty hard. Add 1/3 additional water to cook to make rice softer.

煮饭的技巧
Cooking Techniques

蒸
Steaming

蒸饭的米要先用水浸，捞起米时不用去除全部的水分，只要连同部分水捞起便可，放入蒸笼蒸。

Soak rice for a while before cooking. Do not drain away all water but keep some. Then steam it in a steamer.

炒
Shallow-frying

炒饭时不可将饭压实，要炒松。

Do not press rice tightly during shallow-frying. Keep rice loosen / slacken.

煲仔饭
Hotpot rice

煲好的饭不要即时揭盖，要焗片刻才有香味。
Do not remove cover immediately after cooking. Cover for a while to give aroma.

一餐中各种食物的摄取比例
The proportion of different food intake during a meal

2011年6月美国农业部门（USDA）发表了一套新的健康饮食指南以取代有20年历史的膳食金字塔。这套新饮食指南以一个圆形餐碟做图示，被称作"我的餐碟"（My Plate）。餐碟被分成4份，分别代表4类食物，每餐中有一半是蔬菜及水果，当中蔬菜占较大部分；另外一半则是谷类及蛋白质，而谷类分量比蛋白质稍多。另外还建议一半以上的谷类为全谷物，并且因应年龄需要，每天还要加上1~2份乳制品。

资料来源：chooseMyPlate.gov

看颜色食果蔬
Choose vegetables and fruit according to colour

颜色	植物营养素	果蔬	功效
红	番茄红素	番茄、红菜头、红辣椒、西瓜、西柚	• 降低患癌风险
	花青素	红葡萄、红洋葱、草莓、小红莓、山莓	• 抗氧化及消炎，有助消除体内自由基及发炎因子，活化脑细胞 • 保护心脏
橙/黄	α胡萝卜素、β胡萝卜素	番茄、南瓜、胡萝卜、黄辣椒、木瓜、橘子、杏子、柿子	• 保护视力 • 提升免疫力 • 降低患癌及心脏病风险 • 保持黏膜健康
	玉米黄素	玉米（粟米）、橘子、水蜜桃	• 抗氧化，预防黄斑区受自由基侵害，保护视力
	维生素C	柠檬、橙、菠萝	• 提升免疫力
	叶酸	橙、哈密瓜、芒果	• 负责制造红细胞，预防贫血
绿	叶黄素、玉米黄素	绿豆、芦笋、青椒、菠菜、芥蓝、西兰花、生菜、猕猴桃	• 抗氧化，预防黄斑区受自由基及日光伤害，保护视力 • 降低患癌及心脏病风险
	靛基质、异硫氰酸酯	西兰花、椰菜	• 降低患癌风险
	有机硫化合物（如蒜辣素）	青葱、韭菜	• 降低患癌风险 • 保护心脏
	叶酸	所有绿叶蔬菜，如菠菜、芥蓝等	• 负责制造红细胞，预防贫血
蓝/紫	花青素	茄子、蓝莓、黑莓、紫色葡萄、梅子、无花果	• 抗氧化及消炎，有助消除体内自由基及发炎因子，活化脑细胞 • 保护心脏
白	有机硫化合物（如蒜辣素）	洋葱、蒜头、姜、白萝卜、蘑菇	• 降低患癌风险 • 保护心脏
	钾质	香蕉、马铃薯	• 稳定血压

开始做饭
Let's Start!

美食达人心动试味 / Gourmet's Comments

荷叶要包好，不要令汁料流出。
Wrap lotus leaf properly to avoid sauce spilling out.

Seafood rice in lotus leaf
海鲜荷叶饭

30 分钟 Minutes | 2 人 Persons

Tips

新鲜荷叶有季节性的，干的荷叶比较容易购买，可在干货店购买。
Fresh lotus leaf is a seasonal product. It is easier to buy dry lotus leaf in groceries.

材料　白饭400 克／虾仁4 只／冬菇3 只／青口3 只／鱼柳1 块／荷叶1 张

调味料　生抽1 茶匙／熟油1 茶匙／麻油1/2 茶匙／胡椒粉1/4 茶匙

Ingredients 400g white rice / 4pcs shrimp / 3pcs black mushroom / 3pcs mussel / 1pc fish fillet / 1pc lotus leaf

Seasonings 1tsp light soy sauce / 1tsp cooked oil / 1/2tsp sesame oil / 1/4tsp pepper

做法 Method

1. Soak in hot water to make lotus leaf soft, and pat dry.
2. Soak black mushrooms, remove stem, and dice.
3. Wash fish fillet, mussels and shrimps separately, and dice.
4. Cook black mushrooms, fish fillet, mussels and shrimps in hot water, drain, and add in seasonings.
5. Place lotus leaf flat, add in white rice and other ingredients, wrap to form square shape, and steam for 12 minutes.

1. 荷叶放滚水中浸软，抹干。
2. 冬菇浸软，去蒂，切粒。
3. 鱼柳、青口和虾仁分别洗净，切粒。
4. 煮滚一锅水，加入冬菇、鱼柳、青口和虾仁煮熟，盛起，加入调味料拌匀。
5. 将荷叶摊平，放上白饭，加入各材料，裹成四角形包好，放入蒸笼内，隔水蒸12分钟即成。

蒸饭 Steamed Rice

美食达人心动试味 / Gourmet's Comments

白菜要剁碎些,猪扒要煎得金黄。
Chop Bok Choy into small / fine pieces, and pan-fry pork chop until golden brown.

Shanghai vegetable rice
上海菜饭

⏱ 40 分钟 / Minutes   👥 2 人 / Persons

Tips

1 饭可加入虾米。
You may add dried shrimps into rice.

2 白菜亦可不用锅炒,直接加入米内一同煮。
You may cook Bok Choy with rice together instead of shallow-frying.

材料	猪扒3件 / 白菜100克 / 白饭2碗 / 姜粒1茶匙
腌料	盐1/2茶匙 / 胡椒粉1/2茶匙 / 鸡粉1/2茶匙
调味料	盐少许

Ingredients	3pcs pork chop / 100g Bok Choy / 2 bowls of white rice / 1tsp diced ginger
Marinade	1/2tsp salt / 1/2tsp pepper / 1/2tsp chicken powder
Seasoning	Little salt

做法 / Method

1. Wash Bok Choy, drain and chop.
2. Wash pork chop, use back of knife to chop, and stir in marinade.
3. Heat wok with oil, pan-fry pork chop until golden brown, drain, and chop into pieces.
4. Heat wok with oil again, sauté diced ginger, add in Bok Choy and little salt, shallow-fry until tender, and serve.
5. Put white rice in large bowl, stir in Bok Choy to make vegetable rice, put pork chop on top.

1. 白菜洗净,沥干水分,剁碎。
2. 猪扒洗净,用刀背剁松,加腌料拌匀。
3. 热锅下油,下猪扒煎至金黄熟透,盛起,切块。
4. 再热锅下油,爆香姜粒,加入白菜和少许盐拌炒至软,盛起。
5. 白饭放入大碗中,加入白菜拌匀成菜饭,放上猪扒即成。

美食达人心动试味 / *Gourmet's Comments*

番薯要焗至完全软腍。
Sweet potatoes should be cooked until completely tender.

Sweet potatoes rice
番薯饭

🕐 25 分钟 / Minutes 👥 4 人 / Persons

Tips

可改用白米代替糙米，亦可用一半糙米一半白米。番薯可改为南瓜。

You may use white rice to substitute brown rice, or use 1/2 portion of brown rice and 1/2 portion of white rice; use pumpkin to substitute sweet potatoes.

材料 番薯600 克 / 糙米300 克 / 猪瘦肉150 克 / 葱3 棵 / 虾米2 汤匙

Ingredients 600g sweet potatoes / 300g brown rice / 150g lean pork / 3pcs spring onion / 2tbsps dried shrimp

Method

1. Wash and soak brown rice for 3 hours.
2. Wash other ingredients, dice lean pork, soak dried shrimps, remove root and end part of spring onion and dice, peel sweet potatoes and dice.
3. Heat wok with oil, sauté dried shrimps, add in lean pork and shallow-fry, and stir in sweet potatoes.
4. Cook brown rice in rice cooker with appropriate amount of water. When little water left, add in sauté ingredients, and cook until well done. Sprinkle diced spring onion on top and serve.

做法

1. 糙米淘洗净，预先用水浸 3 小时。
2. 其他材料洗净。猪瘦肉切粒，虾米浸泡，葱切去根部和尾部，切成葱花，番薯去皮，切粒。
3. 热锅下油，下虾米爆香，加入猪瘦肉炒匀，再加入番薯炒匀。
4. 糙米放入电饭煲中，加适量水煮，饭将干水时，加入爆过的材料，焗至所有材料熟透，撒上葱花即成。

美食达人心动试味 / Gourmet's Comments

十谷米一定要浸够时间，否则会太硬。
Mixed grain must be soaked for enough time. Otherwise, they are very hard.

Mixed mushrooms rice
杂菌十谷炊饭

⏱ 20 分钟 / Minutes   👥 4 人 / Persons

Tips

十谷米也可用来煲粥。
You may use mixed grain to make congee.

材料	十谷米300 克 / 猪瘦肉120 克 / 草菇120 克
	秀珍菇（小平菇）120 克 / 冬菇4 只 / 葡萄干1 汤匙 / 蒜蓉1 茶匙
腌料	生粉1/2 茶匙 / 盐1/4 茶匙
调味料	麻油1/2 茶匙 / 鱼露1/2 茶匙

Ingredients	300g mixed grain / 120g lean pork / 120g straw mushrooms / 120g oyster mushrooms / 4pcs black mushroom / 1tbsp raisin / 1tsp garlic puree
Marinade	1/2tsp caltrop starch / 1/4tsp salt
Seasonings	1/2tsp sesame oil / 1/2tsp fish sauce

做法

1. Wash mixed grain and soak for 3 hours. Cook in rice cooker with appropriate amount of water. The amount of water should be 1/3 more than that of cooking white rice.
2. Wash lean pork, dice, and stir in marinade.
3. Soak black mushrooms, remove stem, and shred.
4. Wash straw mushrooms and oyster mushrooms, and blanch.
5. Heat wok with oil. Sauté garlic puree, add in lean pork, then black mushrooms, straw mushrooms, oyster mushrooms and raisins.
6. Mix rice with all ingredients, add seasonings, and serve.

1. 十谷米淘洗净，预先用水浸3小时，放入电饭煲中加水煮熟，水要比平时煲饭的水多1/3。
2. 猪瘦肉洗净，切粒，加腌料拌匀。
3. 冬菇浸软，去蒂，切丝。
4. 草菇、秀珍菇洗净，飞水。
5. 热锅下油，下蒜蓉爆香，加入瘦肉粒炒熟，再加入冬菇、草菇、秀珍菇和葡萄干拌匀。
6. 将所有材料放入饭内，加入调味料拌匀即可。

Steamed Rice

美食达人心动试味 / Gourmet's Comments

淋在饭面的汁料很香,但不要加太多。
Although the sauce is fragrant, do not add too much.

Brown rice with soy sauce chicken
豉油鸡糙米饭

⏱ 25 分钟 / Minutes 👥 2 人 / Persons

Tips

汁料也可以用于浸乳鸽或全只鸡。
The sauce also can be used for soaking pigeon or whole chicken.

材料 鸡腿2 只 / 糙米150 克 / 水360 毫升
汁料 姜2 片 / 葱3 棵 / 酒120 毫升 / 老抽1 杯 / 糖6 汤匙 / 鸡粉1/2茶匙

Ingredients 2pcs chicken leg / 150g brown rice / 360ml water
Sauce 2slices ginger / 3pcs spring onion / 120ml wine / 1 cup of dark soy sauce / 6tbsps sugar / 1/2tsp chicken powder

做法

1. Wash chicken leg and drain. Wash spring onion, remove root and end part, cut.
2. Wash brown rice, Soak for over 30 minutes, and drain.
3. Cook brown rice in rice cooker with appropriate amount of water.
4. Cook sauce in wok, add in chicken leg and cover. Stew for 20 minutes until well done, and serve.
5. Put chicken leg onto rice. Spread some sauce on top.

1. 鸡腿洗净,沥干水分。葱洗净,切去根部和尾部,切段。
2. 糙米淘洗净,用水浸30分钟以上,沥干水分。
3. 糙米放入电饭煲中,加适量水煮至熟。
4. 将汁料放入锅中煮滚,加入鸡腿,盖上锅盖,炆焗20分钟至熟,盛起。
5. 将糙米饭盛起,放上鸡腿,淋上适量汁料即可。

Steamed Rice

美食达人心动试味 / Gourmet's Comments

咸鱼的味道非常香，但不可常吃。
Salted fish smells good. However, we should not always eat this kind of food.

Steamed minced pork with salted fish rice
咸鱼肉饼饭

30 分钟 / Minutes   4 人 / Persons

Tips

煮熟的饭不要即刻开盖，要焗片刻才会有香味。
Do not open cover after cooked. Cover for a while to give aroma.

材料 白米300克 / 半肥瘦猪肉250克 / 咸鱼20克 / 姜4片 / 油少许
腌料 胡椒粉1/2茶匙 / 盐1/3茶匙
调味料 老抽1汤匙 / 生抽1茶匙

Ingredients 300g white rice / 250g semi-fat pork / 20g salted fish / 4 slices ginger / Little oil
Marinade 1/2tsp pepper / 1/3tsp salt
Seasonings 1tbsp dark soy sauce / 1tsp light soy sauce

做法  Method

1. Wash white rice, and drain.
2. Wash ginger, peel, and shred. Wash salted fish, and drain.
3. Wash semi-fat pork, slice and chop, put in large bowl, add in marinade, mix until sticky, and stir in little oil.
4. Cook white rice in rice cooker with appropriate amount of water. Add in semi-fat pork when little water left, add in salted fish and shredded ginger, cover until well done.
5. Sprinkle seasonings, and serve.

1. 白米淘洗净,沥干水分。
2. 姜洗净,用小刀刮去皮,切丝。咸鱼洗净,沥干水分。
3. 半肥瘦猪肉洗净,幼切粗剁,放入大碗中,加入腌料,拌至起胶,加入少许油。
4. 白米放入电饭煲中,加入适量水煮,当饭将干水时将半肥瘦猪肉放在饭面,加上咸鱼和姜丝,盖上盖焗至全熟即可。
5. 食用时淋上调味料。

Steamed Rice

美食达人心动试味 / Gourmet's Comments

要选择比较瘦的腊肠。
Choose preserved lean sausage.

Steamed chicken rice with preserved sausages
腊肠蒸鸡饭

⏱ 30 分钟 / Minutes   👥 3 人 / Persons

Tips
可一起加入冬菇与鸡块。
You may add black mushrooms and chicken pieces together.

材料	光鸡1/2只 / 白米350 克 / 腊肠2 条 / 葱2 棵 / 姜2 片 / 粗盐少许
腌料	生抽1 茶匙 / 姜汁酒1 茶匙 / 油1 茶匙 / 生粉1/2茶匙
调味料	麻油1 茶匙 / 老抽适量

Ingredients	1/2pc chicken / 350g white rice / 2pcs preserved sausage / 2pcs spring onion / 2 slices ginger / Little coarse salt
Marinade	1tsp light soy sauce / 1tsp ginger wine / 1tsp oil / 1/2tsp caltrop starch
Seasonings	1tsp sesame oil / Some dark soy sauce

做法 Method

1. Rub chicken with coarse salt for a while, wash, drain, chop, and marinate for 30 minutes.
2. Wash preserved sausages and drain.
3. Wash ginger, peel and shred. Wash spring onion, remove its root and end part, and dice.
4. Wash white rice, and cook it with preserved sausages in rice cooker with appropriate amount of water. Add in chicken pieces and shredded ginger when little water left. Cover and cook until well done.
5. Slice preserved sausages, add in seasonings and diced spring onion when serve.

1. 光鸡用粗盐略擦，洗净，沥干水分，切块，加入腌料腌30分钟。
2. 腊肠洗净，沥干水分。
3. 姜洗净，用小刀刮去皮，切丝。葱洗净，切去根部和尾部，切成葱花。
4. 白米淘洗净，与腊肠同放入电饭煲中，加入适量水煮，饭将干水时下鸡块和姜丝，盖好盖焗至熟。
5. 食用时将腊肠切片，加入调味料和葱花。

Steamed Rice

美食达人心动试味 | Gourmet's Comments

鸡肉放饭面，一定要有足够时间，令鸡肉煮至熟透。
Put chicken onto rice for enough time to ensure it is well done.

Steamed chicken and black mushrooms rice
冬菇滑鸡片饭

30 分钟 / Minutes
3 人 / Persons

Tips

冬菇浸软后不用去干水分，即可切丝，将带有水分的冬菇一并和鸡片放在饭面。

Need not to drain soaked black mushrooms before shredding. Put soaked black mushrooms and sliced chicken on top of rice.

材料	鸡肉250 克 / 冬菇4 只 / 姜4 片 / 白米350 克
腌料	生抽1 茶匙 / 姜汁酒1 茶匙 / 油1 茶匙 / 胡椒粉1/4 茶匙
调味料	熟油1 茶匙 / 老抽适量

Ingredients	250g chicken / 4pcs black mushroom / 4 slices ginger / 350g white rice
Marinade	1tsp light soy sauce / 1tsp ginger wine / 1tsp oil / 1/4tsp pepper
Seasonings	1tsp cooked oil / Some dark soy sauce

做法 / Method

1. Wash white rice, and drain.
2. Wash chicken, slice, and marinate.
3. Peel ginger, wash and shred. Soak black mushrooms, remove stem and shred.
4. Cook white rice in rice cooker with appropriate amount of water. Add in sliced chicken, black mushrooms and shredded ginger when little water left. Cover and cook until well done.
5. Add in seasonings when serve.

1. 白米淘洗净，沥干水分。
2. 鸡肉洗净，切片，加入腌料拌匀。
3. 姜去皮，洗净，切丝。冬菇浸软，去蒂，切丝。
4. 白米放入电饭煲中，加入适量水煮，饭将干水时下鸡片、冬菇和姜丝，盖好盖焗熟。
5. 食用时加入调味料。

美食达人心动试味 / *Gourmet's Comments*

糙米和黑糯米一定要浸够时间。
Soak brown rice and black glutinous rice for enough time.

Trio tasty rice
三色有味饭

⏱ 45 分钟 / Minutes　　👥 4 人 / Persons

Tips

菇类可改用新鲜茶树菇、冬菇或其他菇类。
You may use fresh tea tree mushrooms, black mushrooms or any other types of mushroom.

材料	腊肠2 条 / 虾米30 克 / 干茶树菇50 克 / 白米150 克 糙米100 克 / 黑糯米100 克 / 葱2 棵 / 上汤300 毫升 水适量 / 盐少许
调味料	生抽2 汤匙 / 老抽1 汤匙 / 油2 茶匙 / 糖1/2 茶匙

Ingredients	2pcs preserved sausage / 30g dried shrimps 50g dried tea tree mushrooms / 150g white rice / 100g brown rice 100g black glutinous rice / 2pcs spring onion / 300ml broth Some water / Little salt
Seasonings	2tbsps light soy sauce / 1tbsp dark soy sauce / 2tsps oil / 1/2tsp sugar

做法 / Method

1. Wash brown rice and black glutinous rice, soak for 2 hours.
2. Wash white rice, mix well 3 types of rice, add in broth and some water, and cook in rice cooker.
3. Wash preserved sausages, steam for 10 minutes over water until well done, slice. Soak dried shrimps and dried tea tree mushrooms, wash and drain.
4. Heat wok with oil. Sauté dried shrimps, preserved sausages and dried tea tree mushrooms, add in little salt. Set aside.
5. Heat wok with oil again. Stir in seasonings and set aside.
6. Mix shallow-fried ingredients and seasonings with rice. Serve.

1. 糙米、黑糯米淘洗净，用水浸2小时。
2. 白米淘洗净。将3种米拌匀，加入上汤和适量水，放入电饭煲内煲熟。
3. 腊肠洗净，隔水蒸10分钟至熟，切片。虾米、干茶树菇浸软，洗净，沥干水分。
4. 热锅下油，爆香虾米、腊肠、干茶树菇，加少许盐拌匀，盛起。
5. 再热锅下油，将调味料拌匀，煮滚备用。
6. 将炒好的材料和调味料加入熟饭拌匀即可。

蒸饭 / Steamed Rice

美食达人心动试味 / Gourmet's Comments

用浸鸡水煮饭时要隔去油分，否则会太油腻。
Remove oil of chicken soup for cooking rice. Otherwise, the rice will be too greasy.

Hainanese chicken rice
海南鸡饭

45 Minutes — 4 Persons

Tips

1. 煮饭时可加入椰汁。
You may add coconut milk when cooking rice.

2. 鸡饭可伴酸菜。酸菜的做法是：将青瓜1条切条，用盐腌片刻，去掉水分，加入白醋3汤匙和糖1¼汤匙，放冰箱冷藏。
Sour vegetables accompany chicken rice is common when serve. Shred 1pc of cucumber and marinate with salt for a while. Drain, add in 3tbsps white vinegar and 1¼tbsps sugar, then put in fridge.

| 材料 | 光鸡1只（约1 500克）/ 白米600 克 / 姜1 块 / 葱2棵 蒜头10 瓣 / 粗盐少许 |
| 调味料 | 盐4 茶匙 + 1 茶匙 / 胡椒粉适量 / 酒适量 / 姜汁适量 |

| Ingredients | 1pc (about 1 500g) chicken / 600g white rice / 1pc ginger 2pcs spring onion / 10 cloves of garlic / Little coarse salt |
| Seasonings | (4+1)tsps salt / Some pepper / Some wine / Some ginger juice |

做法 Method

1. Wash white rice, and drain.

2. Wash ginger, spring onion and garlic. Peel ginger and slice. Remove root and end part of spring onion, and chop. Peel garlic and chop to become puree.

3. Rub chicken with coarse salt for a while, wash, and drain. Remove chicken fat / oil, dice, and set aside.

4. Boil chicken, ginger and spring onion for 10 minutes until chicken is well done. Take chicken out, rub with salt and pepper, let cool and chop into pieces. Keep chicken soup for use.

5. Heat wok with oil. Add in diced chicken fat / oil until dissolved, then sauté garlic puree. Sprinkle wine and ginger juice, stir in white rice and shallow-fry, add in 4tsps salt. Put in rice cooker with appropriate amount of chicken soup, and cook until well done.

1. 白米淘洗净，沥干水分。

2. 姜、葱、蒜头洗净。姜去皮，切片。葱切去根部和尾部，切段。蒜头去衣，剁成蓉。

3. 光鸡用粗盐略擦，洗净，沥干水分。切出鸡油，再切粒，留起待用。

4. 烧滚一大锅水，将光鸡、姜和葱放滚水内浸10分钟，直至光鸡煮熟，捞起，趁热擦上盐和胡椒粉，放凉后切块上碟。浸鸡水留起待用。

5. 热锅下油，加入鸡油粒煮溶，下蒜蓉爆香，潵酒及姜汁，倒入已洗净的白米炒匀，下盐 4 茶匙拌匀，转放入电饭煲内，注入适量浸鸡水煮至饭熟即可。

Steamed Rice

美食达人心动试味 / Gourmet's Comments

每人接受的咸度不同,最好是食用时各自加汁料。
Different people have different tastes. It is better for them to add sauce on their own.

Steamed rice with spareribs, chicken feet and fermented black beans sauce
豉汁排骨凤爪饭

45 分钟 / Minutes   4 人 / Persons

Tips

可将凤爪、排骨和调味料直接放在饭面,这样可节省时间,但味道会比较逊色。
Place chicken feet, spareribs and seasonings onto rice to save time, but it is tasteless.

| 材料 | 炸凤爪4只 / 排骨（可选腩排）300 克 / 白米450 克
红辣椒1只 / 豆豉3 茶匙 / 蒜蓉1 茶匙 / 水适量 |
| 调味料 | 盐1/4 茶匙 / 糖1/4 茶匙 / 胡椒粉1/4 茶匙 / 麻油1/4 茶匙 |
| 汁料 | 老抽适量 / 熟油适量 |

| Ingredients | 4pcs deep-fried chicken feet / 300g spareribs / 450g white rice
1pc red chili / 3tsps fermented black bean(Douchi) / 1tsp garlic puree
Some water |
| Seasonings | 1/4tsp salt / 1/4tsp sugar / 1/4tsp pepper / 1/4tsp sesame oil |
| Sauce | Some dark soy sauce / Some cooked oil |

做法 Method

1. Wash white rice, and drain.
2. Wash deep-fried chicken feet, and remove fingertip.
3. Wash spareribs, and chop into pieces.
4. Wash fermented black beans, chop to become puree. Remove seed of red chili, wash, and shred.
5. Heat wok with oil. Sauté garlic puree and fermented black beans, add in spareribs, deep-fried chicken feet and seasonings, and mix well.
6. Cook rice in rice cooker with appropriate amount of water. Add ingredients when little water left. Cover until well done. Add sauce when serve.

1. 白米淘洗净，沥干水分。
2. 炸凤爪洗净，切去指尖。
3. 排骨洗净，切块。
4. 豆豉洗净，剁蓉。红辣椒去籽，洗净，切丝。
5. 热锅下油，爆香蒜蓉和豆豉，加入排骨、炸凤爪和调味料拌匀。
6. 白米放入电饭煲中，加入适量水煮，饭将干水时将材料放下，盖好盖焗熟，食用时加入汁料。

炒饭 Fried Rice

美食达人心动试味 / Gourmet's Comments

炒饭不要用锅铲压，只要兜炒至松便可。
Do not press rice tightly during pan-frying. Slightly shallow-fry to make rice loosen/slacken.

Western fried rice 西炒饭

⏱ 15 分钟 Minutes 👥 3 人 Persons

Tips

下了番茄酱，如觉得味道太酸，可加少许糖。
You may add little sugar if rice is sour after adding ketchup.

材料 肠仔（火腿肠）3 条 / 青豆 2 汤匙 / 青椒 1/2 个 / 洋葱 1/2 个 / 鸡蛋 1 只 / 白饭 3 碗

调味料 茄汁（番茄酱）4 汤匙 / 盐 1/2 茶匙 / 生抽 1/2 茶匙

Ingredients 3pcs sausage / 2tbsps green beans / 1/2pc green chili 1/2pc onion / 1pc egg / 3 bowls of white rice

Seasonings 4tbsps ketchup / 1/2tsp salt / 1/2tsp light soy sauce

做法 Method

1. Wash sausages and dice. Wash green beans and blanch.
2. Wash green chili, remove seed and dice. Peel onion, wash and dice.
3. Beat the egg in a bowl, whisk egg.
4. Heat wok with oil. Shallow-fry white rice, stir in whisked egg until well done. Set aside.
5. Heat wok with oil again. Sauté onion, add in sausage dices, green chili dices and green beans, then fried white rice, and seasonings at last.

1. 肠仔洗净，切粒。青豆洗净，飞水。
2. 青椒洗净，去籽，切粒。洋葱去衣，洗净，切粒。
3. 鸡蛋打入碗中，打匀成蛋液。
4. 热锅下油，下白饭拌炒，加入蛋液炒至松，盛起。
5. 再热锅下油，炒香洋葱，加入肠仔粒、青椒粒和青豆拌炒，加入已炒的白饭，最后加调味料拌匀即可上碟。

炒饭 Fried Rice

美食达人心动试味 / Gourmet's Comments

叉烧最好买半肥瘦的。
It is better to use semi-fat roasted pork.

Yangzhou fried rice
扬州炒饭

20 Minutes | **4 Persons**

Tips

买叉烧时可请店员将叉烧切粒，可节省一些时间。
You may request the staff at roast shop to dice roasted pork to save time.

材料	虾8 只 / 叉烧120 克 / 白饭3 碗 / 葱3 棵 / 鸡蛋2 只
腌料	生粉1/2 茶匙 / 盐1/4 茶匙 / 胡椒粉1/4 茶匙
调味料	盐1 茶匙 / 生抽1 茶匙

Ingredients	8pcs shrimp / 120g roasted pork / 3 bowls of white rice / 3pcs spring onion / 2pcs egg
Marinade	1/2tsp caltrop starch / 1/4tsp salt / 1/4tsp pepper
Seasonings	1tsp salt / 1tsp light soy sauce

做法 Method

1. Shell shrimps, remove intestine from shrimps, wash and marinate.
2. Dice roasted pork. Wash spring onion, remove root and end part, and dice.
3. Beat the eggs in a bowl, whisk eggs, and stir in a little salt.
4. Heat wok with oil, stir in whisked eggs, pan-fry, dish up and shred.
5. Heat wok with oil again. Add in shrimps, diced roasted pork, then shallow-fry rice add seasonings, shredded eggs and diced spring onion at last.

1. 虾去壳去肠，洗净，加腌料拌匀。
2. 叉烧切粒。葱洗净，切去根部和尾部，切成葱花。
3. 鸡蛋打入碗中，打匀成蛋液，加少许盐拌匀。
4. 热锅下油，下蛋液炒匀，盛起，切丝。
5. 再热锅下油，下虾仁略炒，加入叉烧粒拌炒，再加入白饭和调味料拌炒，最后加入鸡蛋丝和葱花拌匀。

炒饭 / Fried Rice

美食达人心动试味 / Gourmet's Comments

带子不可以炒太久，否则会变韧的。
Do not overcook scallop. Otherwise, it will be tenacious / tough.

Richman's fried rice
有钱佬炒饭

⏱ 20 分钟 / Minutes　　👥 4 人 / Persons

Tips
带子可用冷冻的或新鲜的。
You may use frozen or fresh scallops.

材料	带子4 粒／虾6 只／鸡腿菇40 克／芦笋30 克 本菇（本占地菇）30 克／红甜椒1/2 个／白饭3 碗／蒜蓉1 汤匙
腌料	生粉1/2 茶匙／盐1/4 茶匙／胡椒粉1/4 茶匙
调味料	蚝油1 汤匙／XO酱1 茶匙／麻油1/2 茶匙

Ingredients	4pcs scallop／6pcs shrimp／40g chicken leg mushrooms 30g asparagus／30g shimeji mushrooms／1/2pc red sweet pepper 3 bowls of white rice／1tbsp garlic puree
Marinade	1/2tsp caltrop starch／1/4tsp salt／1/4tsp pepper
Seasonings	1tbsp oyster sauce／1tsp XO sauce／1/2tsp sesame oil

做法 / Method

1. Wash shimeji mushrooms, chicken leg mushrooms and asparagus, then dice and blanch.
2. Wash red sweet pepper, remove seed and dice.
3. Shell shrimps, remove intestine from shrimps and wash. Wash scallops and drain. Marinate shrimps and scallops.
4. Heat wok with oil. Sauté garlic puree, add in shimeji mushrooms, chicken leg mushrooms, asparagus and red sweet pepper, then shrimps and scallops until well done. Set aside
5. Heat wok with oil again. Add in white rice, shallow-fry until loosen/slacken, and stir in above ingredients and seasonings.

1. 本菇、鸡腿菇、芦笋洗净，切粒，飞水。
2. 红甜椒洗净，去籽，切粒。
3. 虾去壳去肠，洗净。带子洗净，沥干水分。虾和带子加腌料拌匀。
4. 热锅下油，爆香蒜蓉，下本菇、鸡腿菇、芦笋和红甜椒略炒，再加入虾和带子炒至全熟，盛起。
5. 再热锅下油，加入白饭炒至松，再加入以上材料和调味料拌匀即成。

Fried Rice

美食达人心动试味 / Gourmet's Comments

咸鱼拆肉时要小心，不要留下鱼骨。
Be careful when removing fish bone, do not leave any bone.

Fried rice with diced chicken and salted fish
咸鱼鸡粒饭

20 Minutes | **4 Persons**

Tips

咸鱼用梅香的会比较甘香。
"Mui hoeng" (soft and wet) salted fish is tastier that the dry ones.

材料	鸡肉250克 / 咸鱼20克 / 鸡蛋2只 / 白饭4碗 / 葱花1汤匙 / 姜丝1汤匙 / 姜粒 1 茶匙 / 蒜蓉1 茶匙
腌料	盐1/2 茶匙 / 胡椒粉1/2 茶匙
调味料	生抽1 茶匙 / 老抽1 茶匙 / 盐1/2 茶匙

Ingredients	250g chicken / 20g salted fish / 2pcs egg / 4 bowls of white rice / 1tbsp diced spring onion / 1tbsp shredded ginger / 1tsp diced ginger / 1tsp garlic puree
Marinade	1/2tsp salt / 1/2tsp pepper
Seasonings	1tsp light soy sauce / 1tsp dark soy sauce / 1/2tsp salt

做法 / Method

1. Wash chicken, dice and marinate.

2. Heat wok with oil. Parboil chicken and drain.

3. Wash salted fish and drain. Put on plate, sprinkle shredded ginger on top, steam over water for 10 minutes. Let cool and remove bone.

4. Beat the eggs in a bowl, whisk eggs and stir in a little salt. Heat wok with oil, add whisked eggs to stir well. Dish up and shred.

5. Heat wok with oil. Sauté diced ginger and garlic puree, add in white rice and shallow-fry until loosen/slacken. Add in chicken, salted fish and shredded eggs, then seasonings and diced spring onion. Serve.

1. 鸡肉洗净，切粒，加腌料拌匀。

2. 烧热油锅，将鸡肉泡油，沥干油分备用。

3. 咸鱼洗净，沥干水分。咸鱼放碟上，铺上姜丝，隔水蒸10分钟，待凉拆肉。

4. 鸡蛋打入碗中，打匀成蛋液，加少许盐拌匀。热锅下油，下蛋液炒匀，盛起，切丝。

5. 热锅下油，爆香姜粒和蒜蓉，下白饭炒至松，将鸡肉、咸鱼和鸡蛋丝回锅，加入调味料拌匀，撒上葱花即可上碟。

炒饭 Fried Rice

美食达人心动试味 / Gourmet's Comments

牛肉要炒至松开,不要黏结在一起。
Shallow-fry beef until loosen/slacken, do not stick together.

Fried rice with beef
生炒牛肉饭

⏱ 20 分钟 / Minutes   👥 4 人 / Persons

Tips

不可以用盐腌牛肉,否则会变韧。
Do not use salt to marinate beef. Otherwise, beef will be tenacious / tough.

材料	牛肉250 克 / 鸡蛋1 只 / 白饭4 碗 / 葱3 棵 / 蒜蓉1 汤匙
腌料	生油1 汤匙（后下）/ 生抽1 茶匙 / 水1 茶匙 / 生粉1 茶匙 / 胡椒粉1/4 茶匙
调味料	生抽1 茶匙 / 老抽1 茶匙 / 盐1/2 茶匙

Ingredients	250g beef / 1pc egg / 4 bowls of white rice / 3pcs spring onion / 1tbsp garlic puree
Marinade	1tbsp oil (add at last) / 1tsp light soy sauce / 1tsp water / 1tsp caltrop starch / 1/4tsp pepper
Seasonings	1tsp light soy sauce / 1tsp dark soy sauce / 1/2tsp salt

做法 / Method

1. Wash beef, mince, marinate, and add oil.
2. Wash spring onion, remove root and end part, dice.
3. Beat the egg in a bowl, whisk egg.
4. Heat wok with oil. Sauté garlic puree, add in beef and shallow-fry until medium rare. Set aside.
5. Heat wok with oil again. Add in white rice and whisked egg, then beef, diced spring onion and seasonings. Cook well and serve.

1. 牛肉洗净，剁碎，加腌料拌匀，下生油盖面。
2. 葱洗净，切去根部和尾部，切成葱花。
3. 鸡蛋打入碗中，打匀成蛋液。
4. 热锅下油，爆香蒜蓉，下牛肉炒至五成熟，盛起。
5. 再热锅下油，下白饭和蛋液炒透，将牛肉回锅，加葱花和调味料炒匀即可上碟。

炒饭
Fried Rice

美食达人心动试味 / Gourmet's Comments

糯米要不停炒才不会黏锅。
Non-stop shallow-fry glutinous rice to avoid it sticking to the wok.

Stir-fried glutinous rice
生炒糯米饭

⏱ 30 分钟 / Minutes   👥 4 人 / Persons

Tips

1 可随意加减水和鸡汤的分量。
You may add more or less water and chicken soup.

2 糯米需要炒10~15分钟。
Shallow-fry glutinous rice for 10-15 minutes.

材料	腊肉1条 / 腊肠3条 / 虾米80克 / 糯米600克 / 芫荽1棵 / 葱1棵 / 水1杯
调味料	鸡汤1杯 / 盐1茶匙 / 老抽1茶匙 / 酒1茶匙 / 麻油1/2茶匙

Ingredients	1pc preserved pork / 3pcs preserved sausage / 80g dried shrimps / 600g glutinous rice / 1pc parsley / 1pc spring onion / 1 cup of water
Seasonings	1 cup of chicken soup / 1tsp salt / 1tsp dark soy sauce / 1tsp wine / 1/2tsp sesame oil

做法 / Method

1. Wash glutinous rice, and soak for 2-3 hours, and drain.

2. Wash preserved pork and preserved sausage, drain, steam over water for 10 minutes, and dice.

3. Soak dried shrimps, wash and drain. Wash parsley and spring onion, remove root and end part, and dice respectively.

4. Heat wok with oil. Sauté preserved pork, preserved sausage and dried shrimps, stir in sesame oil, sprinkle wine. Set aside.

5. Heat wok with 6-7tbsps oil. Add in glutinous rice, shallow-fry until loosen and sticky. Add little water by batch, shallow-fry glutinous rice until almost done. Stir in little chicken soup by batch until glutinous rice is well done. Add in preserved pork, preserved sausage, dried shrimps, diced parsley, diced spring onion and dark soy sauce. Mix well and serve.

1. 糯米淘洗净，预先用水浸2～3小时，沥干水分。

2. 腊肉、腊肠洗净，沥干水分。隔水蒸10分钟，切粒。

3. 虾米浸软，洗净，沥干水分。芫荽和葱洗净，切去根部和尾部，分别切成芫荽碎和葱花。

4. 热锅下油，爆香腊肉、腊肠和虾米，加麻油拌匀，溅酒，盛起备用。

5. 再热锅下油，下油6～7汤匙，加入糯米轻力炒松，炒至有黏性，将水逐少洒下，炒至糯米八成熟，再逐少洒下鸡汤至糯米全熟，下蒸好的腊肉、腊肠、虾米、芫荽碎、葱花和老抽拌匀即可。

炒饭 / Fried Rice

美食达人心动试味 / Gourmet's Comments

老抽不可加太多，否则炒饭的颜色太深，不美观。

Do not add too much dark soy sauce. Otherwise, the colour of fried rice is too dark and the outlook is not beautiful.

Fried rice with pork floss, diced ginger and egg white
肉松姜粒蛋白炒饭

20 Minutes / 20 分钟
3 Persons / 3 人

Tips

鸡蛋白不可炒得太久。
Do not stir-fry egg white for too long time.

材料	猪瘦肉80 克 / 鸡蛋白3 只 / 姜粒2 茶匙 / 葱4 棵 / 白饭4 碗
腌料	生粉1/2 茶匙 / 盐1/4 茶匙 / 糖1/4 茶匙
调味料	盐1/2 茶匙 / 鸡粉1/2 茶匙 / 老抽1/4 茶匙

Ingredients	80g lean pork / 3pcs egg white / 2tsps diced ginger / 4pcs spring onion / 4 bowls of white rice
Marinade	1/2tsp caltrop starch / 1/4tsp salt / 1/4tsp sugar
Seasonings	1/2tsp salt / 1/2tsp chicken powder / 1/4tsp dark soy sauce

做法 / Method

1. Wash lean pork, drain, slice and chop, marinate for 15 minutes.
2. Wash spring onion, remove root and end part, dice.
3. Whisk egg white in large bowl.
4. Heat wok with 1tbsp oil. Add in egg white, stir-fry until coagulated. Set aside.
5. Heat wok with oil again, add in minced pork and diced ginger, stir-fry until pork is well done. Add in white rice and shallow-fry until heat, then add in seasonings, egg white, sprinkle diced spring onion and serve.

1. 猪瘦肉洗净，沥干水分。幼切粗剁，加入腌料腌15分钟。
2. 葱洗净，切去根部和尾部，切葱花。
3. 鸡蛋白放大碗中打成蛋液。
4. 烧热锅，下油约1汤匙，加入鸡蛋白炒至凝固，盛起。
5. 再热锅下油，下猪肉碎和姜粒炒至猪肉熟，加入白饭炒匀至热，下调味料拌匀，将鸡蛋白回锅，撒下葱花即可。

炒饭 Fried Rice

美食达人心动试味 / Gourmet's Comments

菠萝要沥干水分才加入,否则炒饭会太湿。
Drain away excess water of pineapple. Otherwise, the fried rice will be too wet.

Pineapple fried rice
菠萝炒饭

⏱ 20 分钟 / Minutes 👥 4 人 / Persons

Tips

菠萝要在炒好其他材料后才下,味道才会甜。
Add pineapple at last when all other ingredients are well done to give sweet flavour.

材料	虾12 只／菠萝2 片／猪瘦肉100 克／洋葱1/2 个／鸡蛋1 只 白饭3 碗／速冻胡萝卜粒、青豆、玉米粒各 20 克
腌料	胡椒粉1/2 茶匙／生粉1/2 茶匙／盐1/8 茶匙
调味料	生抽1 茶匙／老抽1/2 茶匙／盐1/2 茶匙／糖1/2 茶匙

Ingredients	12pcs shrimp／2pcs pineapple／100g lean pork／1/2pc onion 1pc egg／3 bowls of white rice 20g frozen carrot dices, green beans and corn kernels respectively
Marinade	1/2tsp pepper／1/2tsp caltrop starch／1/8tsp salt
Seasonings	1tsp light soy sauce／1/2tsp dark soy sauce／1/2tsp salt 1/2tsp sugar

做法 / Method

1. Shell shrimps, remove intestine from shrimps, wash and stir in 1/2 portion of marinade.
2. Wash lean pork, dice and stir in the rest of marinade.
3. Peel onion, wash and cut into pieces. Cut pineapple into pieces. Whisk egg in a large bowl.
4. Wash carrot dices, green beans and corn kernels, drain, blanch, and dish up, and drain again.
5. Heat wok with oil, add in white rice and egg, stir-fry until loosen/slacken. Set aside.
6. Heat wok with oil again. Sauté onion, add in lean pork and shrimps, then carrot dices, green beans, corn kernels, white rice, seasonings and pineapple. Stir-fry until well done. Serve.

1. 虾去壳去肠，洗净，加一半腌料拌匀。
2. 猪瘦肉洗净，切粒，加另一半腌料拌匀。
3. 洋葱去衣，洗净，切块。菠萝切块。鸡蛋放入大碗中打成蛋液。
4. 胡萝卜粒、青豆、玉米粒洗净，沥干水分，飞水，盛起，再沥干水分。
5. 热锅下油，下白饭和鸡蛋炒松，盛起备用。
6. 再热锅下油，爆香洋葱，下瘦肉粒和虾拌炒，再加入胡萝卜粒、青豆、玉米粒炒匀，将白饭回锅，加入调味料和菠萝拌匀即可。

炒饭 Fried Rice

美食达人心动试味 / Gourmet's Comments

两种汁的红白色要分明，不要混在一起。
Red and white sauce should be clearly shown. Do not mix them together.

Duo-colour fried rice
鸳鸯炒饭

⏱ 30 分钟 / Minutes 👥 4 人 / Persons

Tips

1 如用新鲜蟹会更鲜味。
Fresh crab meat gives better flavour.

2 蟹肉汁料不可炒太久，否则鸡蛋白会太"老"。
Do not cook sauce of crab meat for too long time. Otherwise, egg white will be overcooked.

材料	蟹肉40克 / 虾6只 / 鸡胸肉丝1份 / 洋葱丝1份 / 鸡蛋2只 / 白饭3碗
调味料	生粉1/2茶匙 / 盐1/4茶匙 / 胡椒粉1/8茶匙
鸡丝汁料	番茄酱4汤匙 / 糖1½茶匙 / 生粉2/3茶匙 / 盐1/2茶匙 / 胡椒粉1/4茶匙 / 水50毫升
蟹肉汁料	鲜奶120毫升 / 鸡蛋白1只 / 生粉2/3茶匙 / 盐1/2茶匙 / 糖1/2茶匙 / 胡椒粉1/4茶匙

Ingredients	40g crab meat / 6pcs shrimp / 1pc shredded chicken breast / 1pc shredded onion / 2pcs egg / 3 bowls of white rice
Seasonings	1/2tsp caltrop starch / 1/4tsp salt / 1/8tsp pepper
Sauce of shredded chicken	4tbsps ketchup / 1½tsp sugar / 2/3tsp caltrop starch / 1/2tsp salt / 1/4tsp pepper / 50ml water
Sauce of crab meat	120ml fresh milk / 1pc egg white / 2/3tsp caltrop starch / 1/2tsp salt / 1/2tsp sugar / 1/4tsp pepper

做法 Method

1. Wash crab meat, drain and marinate with a pinch of salt. Shell shrimps, remove intestine from shrimps, wash and drain.

2. Heat wok with oil. Add in shrimp and 1/2 portion of seasonings, stir-fry. Set aside.

3. Heat wok with oil. Add in chicken and the rest of seasonings, parboil and set aside. Heat wok with oil again and sauté shredded onion. Set aside.

4. Whisk eggs in a large bowl. Heat wok with oil. Stir-fry eggs until well done, and dice shred. Add in white rice and shredded eggs, shallow-fry, and serve.

5. Heat wok with oil. Add in sauce of shredded chicken, cook until texture is viscous / thick. Add in shredded onion and shredded chicken. Spread onto one side of rice.

6. Heat wok with oil again. Add in sauce of crab meat, cook until texture is viscous / thick. Add in crab meat and shrimps. Spread onto the other side of rice.

1. 蟹肉洗净，沥干水分，加少许盐略腌。虾去壳去肠，洗净，沥干水分。

2. 热锅下油，下虾和一半调味料炒熟，盛起。

3. 热锅下油，加鸡肉和另一半调味料，泡油至半熟后沥油盛起备用。再热锅下油，下洋葱丝炒香，盛起。

4. 鸡蛋放入大碗中打成蛋液。热锅下油，下鸡蛋液拌炒至熟，盛起切碎丝。再加入白饭和鸡蛋丝同炒匀，上碟。

5. 热锅下油，下鸡丝汁料煮至浓稠，混入洋葱丝和鸡丝拌匀，淋在一半饭面上。

6. 再热锅下油，下蟹肉汁料煮至浓稠，加入蟹肉和虾肉拌匀，淋在另一半饭面上便成。

炒饭 Fried Rice

美食达人心动试味 / Gourmet's Comments

炒好的饭不要太干,而是有汁且比较湿润的。
The fried rice should be pretty wet rather than too dry.

Fujian fried rice
福建炒饭

⏱ 20 分钟 / Minutes　　👥 4 人 / Persons

Tips

福建炒饭的汁料会比较深色,要用老抽增加颜色。
The sauce of Fujian fried rice is darker. Therefore, dark soy sauce is used to increase rice colour.

材料	鸡肉120克／烧鸭肉120克／虾8只／带子4只／冬菇4只 鸡蛋2只／芥蓝梗2棵／白饭3碗
海鲜腌料	生粉1/2茶匙／盐1/4茶匙／胡椒粉1/4茶匙
鸡肉腌料	生粉1/2茶匙／盐1/4茶匙
调味料	鸡汤1/2杯／蚝油1茶匙／老抽1/2茶匙／胡椒粉1/4茶匙
芡汁	生粉1茶匙／水1汤匙

Ingredients	120g chicken / 120g roasted duck meat / 8pcs shrimp 4pcs scallop / 4pcs black mushroom / 2pcs egg 2pcs Chinese kale stem / 3 bowls of white rice
Seafood Marinade	1/2tsp caltrop starch / 1/4tsp salt / 1/4tsp pepper
Chicken Marinade	1/2tsp caltrop starch / 1/4tsp salt
Seasonings	1/2cup of chicken soup / 1tsp oyster sauce 1/2tsp dark soy sauce / 1/4tsp pepper
Thickening	1tsp caltrop starch / 1tbsp water

做法 / Method

1. Shell shrimps, remove intestine from shrimps and wash. Wash scallops. Marinate shrimps and scallops with seafood marinade.

2. Wash chicken, remove skin, dice and stir in chicken marinade.

3. Wash Chinese kale stem and dice. Dice roasted duck meat.

4. Soak black mushrooms, remove stem and dice. Whisk eggs in a large bowl.

5. Heat wok with oil. Add in white rice and whisked eggs, stir-fry. Set aside.

6. Heat wok with oil again. Add in diced chicken and diced black mushrooms. Stir-fry until chicken is almost well done. Add in shrimps and scallops, diced roasted duck meat and diced Chinese kale stem, then seasonings, cook for a while, stir in thickening, and spread onto rice.

1. 虾去壳去肠，洗净，带子洗净，虾和带子加海鲜腌料拌匀。

2. 鸡肉洗净，去皮，切块，加鸡肉腌料拌匀。

3. 芥蓝梗洗净，切粒，烧鸭肉切块。

4. 冬菇浸软，去蒂，切粒。鸡蛋放入大碗中打成蛋液。

5. 热锅下油，下白饭和蛋液炒匀，上碟备用。

6. 再热锅下油，加入鸡肉粒和冬菇粒炒至鸡肉八成熟，加入虾和带子拌匀，再加入烧鸭块和芥蓝粒，然后加入调味料煮滚，最后下芡汁拌匀，淋在炒饭面即可。

炒饭 / Fried Rice

美食达人心动试味 / Gourmet's Comments

海鲜类飞水后已熟了，所以加入饭内炒时不用炒得太久。

Seafood is well done after blanching. It is unnecessary to stir-fry for a long period of time after adding to rice.

Fried rice with red curry seafood
红咖喱海鲜炒饭

20 分钟 / Minutes　**4 人 / Persons**

Tips

芥蓝可改为青、红甜椒。

You may use green sweet pepper and red sweet pepper to substitute Chinese kale.

材料	青口4只 / 虾仁4只 / 鱼柳1条 / 芥蓝梗2棵 / 白饭3碗 红咖喱酱2茶匙 / 蒜蓉1茶匙
腌料	盐少许 / 胡椒粉少许 / 生粉少许
调味料	生抽1/2茶匙 / 盐1/2茶匙 / 糖1/4茶匙

Ingredients	4pcs mussel / 4pcs shrimp / 1pc fish fillet / 2pcs Chinese kale stem 3 bowls of white rice / 2tsps red curry paste / 1tsp garlic puree
Marinade	Little salt / Little pepper / Little caltrop starch
Seasonings	1/2tsp light soy sauce / 1/2tsp salt / 1/4tsp sugar

做法 / Method

1. Wash shrimps, mussels and fish fillet respectively, dice, blanch, drain and marinate.
2. Wash Chinese kale stem, dice and blanch.
3. Heat wok with oil. Sauté garlic puree and red curry paste, add in white rice and stir-fry until loosen/slacken, then add in seasonings, shrimps, mussels and fish fillet, stir-fry for a while, add diced Chinese kale at last. Serve.

1. 虾仁、青口、鱼柳分别洗净，切粒，飞水，沥干水分，加入腌料拌匀。
2. 芥蓝梗洗净，切粒，飞水。
3. 热锅下油，爆香蒜蓉和红咖喱酱，加入白饭炒至松散热透，下调味料拌匀，再加入虾仁、青口、鱼柳略炒，下芥蓝粒炒匀即可上碟。

炒饭 / Fried Rice

美食达人心动试味 / Gourmet's Comments

烟三文鱼已有咸味，不用再另加调味料。
As smoked salmon has salty flavour, it is unnecessary to add other seasonings.

Japanese seafood fried rice
日式海鲜炒饭

20 分钟 / Minutes
4 人 / Persons

Tips

香草可用百里香或混合香草。
You may use thyme or mixed herbs.

材料　烟三文鱼100 克 / 鳗鱼100 克 / 虾仁100 克 / 蟹子3 汤匙
鸡蛋1 只 / 白饭3 碗 / 香草少许

调味料　鳗鱼烧汁3 茶匙 / 盐1/2 茶匙 / 糖1/2 茶匙 / 胡椒粉1/4 茶匙

Ingredients　100g smoked salmon / 100g eel / 100g shrimps / 3tbsps crab roes
1pc egg / 3 bowls of white rice / Little herb

Seasonings　3tsps eel BBQ sauce / 1/2tsp salt / 1/2tsp sugar / 1/4tsp pepper

做法 Method

1. Wash shrimps and dice. Dice smoked salmon and eel.

2. Beat the egg in a large bowl, whisk egg.

3. Heat wok with oil. Add in shrimps, stir-fry until well done, add in smoked salmon, eel, herb and seasonings. Set aside.

4. Heat wok with oil again. Add in whisked egg, stir-fry until loosen/slacken, add in white rice and cook until well done, stir in seafood and crab roes. Serve.

1. 虾仁洗净，切粒。烟三文鱼、鳗鱼切粒。

2. 鸡蛋打入大碗中，打匀成蛋液。

3. 热锅下油，加入虾仁炒熟，再下烟三文鱼、鳗鱼、香草和调味料拌匀，盛起。

4. 再热锅下油，下蛋液炒散，加入白饭炒至饭热透，将炒好的海鲜回锅，加入蟹子拌匀即可上碟。

炒饭 / Fried Rice

美食达人心动试味 / Gourmet's Comments

蚝油不要下太多，只要用来提味便可。
Do not add too much oyster sauce.

Fried rice with curry beef short ribs
牛仔骨咖喱炒饭

25 分钟 / Minutes
3 人 / Persons

Tips

牛仔骨不要煎得太熟。
Do not overcook beef short ribs.

材料　牛仔骨320 克 / 番茄2 个 / 洋葱1 个 / 速冻胡萝卜粒1 汤匙
　　　速冻青豆1 汤匙 / 白饭3 碗 / 蒜蓉2 茶匙 / 咖喱酱2 茶匙
　　　鸡蛋1 只
腌料　生抽1 茶匙 / 糖1/2 茶匙 / 黑胡椒粉1/2 茶匙 / 生粉1/2 茶匙
调味料　蚝油3茶匙 / 鸡粉1/2 茶匙 / 黑胡椒粉1/2 茶匙

Ingredients: 320g beef short ribs / 2pcs tomato / 1pc onion / 1tbsp frozen carrot dices / 1tbsp frozen green beans / 3 bowls of white rice / 2tsps garlic puree / 2tsps curry paste / 1pc egg
Marinade: 1tsp light soy sauce / 1/2tsp sugar / 1/2tsp black pepper / 1/2tsp caltrop starch
Seasonings: 3tsps oyster sauce / 1/2tsp chicken powder / 1/2tsp black pepper

做法 Method

1. Wash beef short ribs and marinate.
2. Peel onion, wash and shred. Wash tomatoes and dice.
3. Wash carrot dices and green beans, and blanch.
4. Beat the egg in a large bowl, whisk egg.
5. Heat wok with oil. Add in white rice and whisked egg, and set aside. Heat wok with oil again, pan-fry beef short ribs, and set aside.
6. Heat wok with oil again. Sauté garlic puree and curry paste. Add in onion shreds, tomato dices, then seasonings, carrot dices, green beans, beef short ribs and egg rice. Stir-fry until well done.

1. 牛仔骨洗净，加腌料拌匀。
2. 洋葱去衣，洗净，切丝。番茄洗净，切粒。
3. 胡萝卜粒、青豆洗净，飞水。
4. 鸡蛋打入大碗中，打匀成蛋液。
5. 热锅下油，下白饭和蛋液炒匀，盛起备用。再热锅下油，下牛仔骨煎至金黄，盛起备用。
6. 再热锅下油，爆蒜蓉和咖喱酱，下洋葱丝、番茄粒拌炒，再加入调味料、胡萝卜粒和青豆拌匀，将牛仔骨回锅，加入鸡蛋饭拌匀即可。

Other 其他

美食达人心动试味 / Gourmet's Comments

红葱头和蒜头不要爆得太过，否则会变黑。
Do not over sauté shallot and garlic. Otherwise, they will be burnt.

Taiwanese pork rice
台式卤肉饭

20 分钟 / Minutes　　3 人 / Persons

Tips

红葱头可以炸香，食用时洒在饭面，增加香味。
You may deep-fry shallot, and spread onto rice to increase flavour.

材料	免治猪肉（猪肉馅）300 克 / 冬菇4 只 / 白饭3 碗 / 红葱头4 粒 / 蒜头2 瓣 / 虾米1/2 茶匙
腌料	糖1/2 茶匙 / 生抽1/2 茶匙 / 生粉1/2 茶匙 / 盐1/4 茶匙
调味料	老抽150 毫升 / 酒1 茶匙 / 胡椒粉1/2 茶匙 / 糖1/2 茶匙 / 水100 毫升

Ingredients	300g minced pork / 4pcs black mushroom / 3 bowls of white rice / 4pcs shallot / 2 cloves of garlic / 1/2tsp dried shrimps
Marinade	1/2tsp sugar / 1/2tsp light soy sauce / 1/2tsp caltrop starch / 1/4tsp salt
Seasonings	150ml dark soy sauce / 1tsp wine / 1/2tsp pepper / 1/2tsp sugar / 100ml water

做法 Method

1. Keep white rice warm.
2. Marinate minced pork.
3. Peel shallot and garlic, and chop into puree.
4. Soak dried shrimps, wash and chop. Soak black mushrooms, remove stem and dice.
5. Heat wok with oil. Sauté shallot puree and garlic puree. Add in dried shrimps and diced black mushrooms, stir-fry, then minced pork and seasonings, cook until little sauce left. Spread onto rice and serve.

1. 白饭保温。
2. 免治猪肉加腌料拌匀。
3. 红葱头、蒜头去衣，切蓉。
4. 虾米浸软，洗净，切碎。冬菇浸软，洗净，去蒂，切粒。
5. 热锅下油，爆香红葱头蓉和蒜茸，加入虾米和冬菇粒拌炒，加入免治猪肉和调味料煮至汁稍干，淋在饭面上即可。

其他 Other

美食达人心动试味 / Gourmet's Comments

猪扒要煎至金黄和全熟,不要煎焦。
Pan-fry pork chop until golden brown and well done. Do not overcook and make it burnt.

Baked pork chop rice
焗猪扒饭

⏱ 30 分钟 / Minutes   👥 3 人 / Persons

Tips

用刀背剁猪扒的一面即可剁松,剁过的猪扒就不会变韧。
Use back of knife to chop one side of pork chop is enough. After chopping, the pork chop will not be tenacious/tough.

材料	猪扒6件 / 红甜椒1/2个 / 青椒1/2个 / 洋葱1/2个 / 白饭3碗 / 蒜蓉2茶匙
腌料	糖1茶匙 / 生抽1茶匙 / 生粉1茶匙 / 盐1/2茶匙
汁料	蚝油1茶匙 / 喼汁1/2茶匙 / 黑胡椒粉1/2茶匙 / 水100毫升

Ingredients	6pcs pork chop / 1/2pc red sweet pepper / 1/2pc green chili / 1/2pc onion / 3 bowls of white rice / 2tsps garlic puree
Marinade	1tsp sugar / 1tsp light soy sauce / 1tsp caltrop starch / 1/2tsp salt
Sauce	1tsp oyster sauce / 1/2tsp Worcestershire sauce / 1/2tsp black pepper / 100ml water

做法 Method

1. Wash pork chop, use back of knife to chop, and marinate.
2. Wash onion, peel and cut into pieces. Wash red sweet pepper and green chili, remove seed and cut into pieces.
3. Heat wok with oil. Pan-fry pork chop until golden brown on both sides. Set aside.
4. Put white rice on glass plate, and place pork chop on top.
5. Heat wok with oil again, and sauté garlic puree and onion. Add in red sweet pepper and green chili, stir in sauce and cook for a while, and spread onto pork chop. Bake in preheated oven at 180°C until golden brown.

1. 猪扒洗净，用刀背剁松，加入腌料拌匀。
2. 洋葱洗净，去衣，切块。红甜椒、青椒分别洗净，去籽，切块。
3. 热锅下油，下猪扒煎至两面金黄，盛起备用。
4. 白饭放在玻璃深碟，铺上猪扒。
5. 再热锅下油，爆香蒜蓉和洋葱，加入红甜椒和青椒拌匀，加入汁料煮片刻，淋在猪扒上，放入预热180℃的焗炉内，焗至金黄色即可。

其他 / Other

美食达人心动试味 / Gourmet's Comments

牛腩经长时间炆制，又软又入味。
Beef brisket is tender and tasteful after long time stew.

Rice with stewed spicy beef brisket
柱侯炆牛腩饭

2 小时 / Hours

4~6 人 / Persons

Tips

牛腩要原块炆，如切小件后再炆，会缩小及走失肉汁。
Beef brisket should be stewed in large chunks. Small cut will lost "juice" and make the meat to be dry and hard.

材料	牛腩900克 / 白饭4~6碗 / 蒜头1~2瓣 / 姜3~4片 / 柱侯酱2茶匙 八角2粒 / 香叶1片 / 冰糖40克 / 水3升 / 玫瑰露酒1~2茶匙
芡汁	老抽2茶匙 / 生粉2茶匙 / 水4汤匙 / 盐1茶匙

Ingredients	900g beef brisket / 4-6 bowls of white rice / 1-2 cloves of garlic 3-4 slices ginger / 2tsps Chu-hau sauce / 2pcs star aniseed 1pc bay leaf / 40g rock sugar / 3L water / 1-2tsps rose wine
Thickening	2tsps dark soy sauce / 2tsps caltrop starch / 4tbsps water / 1tsp salt

做法 / Method

1. Remove the fat from the beef brisket, wash the beef brisket thoroughly, blanch, rinse and then set aside.

2. Heat wok with 1-2tbsps oil. Sauté garlic, ginger and Chu-hau sauce, and stir-fry beef brisket. Add in water, star aniseed, bay leaf and rock sugar, and boil it. Then turn the heat to medium level and stew it for 1-1½ hours until the meat become tenders. Add in rose wine and boil it. Turn off the heat and leave it for 10-15 minutes.

3. Heat wok again. Pour in the thickening ingredients and cook until thickens.

4. Serve the beef brisket with white rice and vegetables.

1. 牛腩去掉脂肪部分，洗净飞水，过冷，备用。

2. 热锅下油，烧熟1~2汤匙油，加入蒜头、姜片和柱侯酱爆透，放入牛腩炒透，加入水、八角、香叶和冰糖煮滚，改中火炆煮1~1½小时，直至炆脸，加入玫瑰露酒，煮滚，熄火焗10~15分钟。

3. 再次加热，埋入芡汁煮至浓稠，即成。

4. 吃时与白饭和时菜一同享用。

其他 / Other

美食达人心动试味 / Gourmet's Comments

蚬肉很快熟，不要炒得太久，否则会缩得很小。
The cooking time of clam is short. Do not shallow-fry it for too long time. Otherwise, it will shrink and become very small.

Clams rice
蚬肉拌饭

⏱ 15 分钟 / Minutes　　👥 2 人 / Persons

Tips

可购买新鲜的蚬，但要先用水浸2小时，令蚬吐出沙，再汆水，然后取出蚬肉。
If fresh clam is used, soak it for 2 hours to remove sand and mud, then blanch and remove clam shell.

材料	蚬肉200 克／白饭2 碗／蒜蓉2 汤匙／速冻青豆1 汤匙
调味料	酒1/2汤匙／忌廉汤100 毫升／水120毫升

Ingredients	200g clams／2 bowls of white rice／2tbsps garlic puree／1tbsp frozen green beans
Seasonings	1/2tbsp wine／100ml cream soup／120ml water

做法 Method

1. Wash clams and drain.
2. Blanch green beans and drain.
3. Put white rice on plate.
4. Heat wok with oil. Sauté garlic puree, add in clams, sprinkle wine, stir in green beans, cream soup and water. Cook until well done. Spread onto white rice and serve.

1. 蚬肉洗净，沥干水分。
2. 青豆飞水，沥干水分。
3. 白饭放在深碟。
4. 热锅下油，爆香蒜蓉，加入蚬肉炒匀，溅酒，加入青豆、忌廉汤和水，煮滚，淋在饭面上即可。

其他 Other

美食达人心动试味 / Gourmet's Comments

牛肉不要煎得太久，否则会变韧。
Do not pan-fry beef for too long time. Otherwise, it will be tenacious/tough.

Korean stone rice
韩式石头锅饭

⏱ 20 分钟 / Minutes 👥 2 人 / Persons

Tips

新买回来的石头锅要先用水浸1小时以上。
Soak new stone pot in water over 1 hour before use.

材料	牛肉薄片200 克 / 青瓜1/2 条 / 胡萝卜1/3 根 / 韩国泡菜50 克 / 大豆芽40 克 / 本菇（本占地菇）30 克 / 鸡蛋黄1 只 / 白饭2 碗
腌料	生抽1茶匙 / 胡椒粉1/4 茶匙
调味料	韩式辣椒酱1 汤匙 / 生抽1 茶匙 / 麻油1/2 茶匙

Ingredients	200g sliced beef / 1/2pc cucumber / 1/3pc carrot / 50g kimchi / 40g soybean sprouts / 30g shimeji mushrooms / 1pc egg yolk / 2 bowls of white rice
Marinade	1tsp light soy sauce / 1/4tsp pepper
Seasonings	1tbsp Korean chili sauce / 1tsp light soy sauce / 1/2tsp sesame oil

做法 Method

1. Wash beef, drain and marinate.
2. Wash shimeji mushrooms and soybean sprouts, drain. Wash cucumber and carrot, drain, shave and shred.
3. Heat wok with oil. Pan-fry beef and set aside.
4. Heat wok with oil again. Add in shredded carrot, shredded cucumber, shimeji mushrooms, soybean sprouts, kimchi and seasonings, serve.
5. Put white rice into stone pot. Spread stir-fried beef and other ingredients on top.
6. Heat stone pot over stove. Cook until clattering sound is heard and rice is slightly burnt. Add egg yolk on top and serve.

1. 牛肉洗净，沥干水分，加腌料拌匀。
2. 本菇、大豆芽洗净，沥干水分。青瓜、胡萝卜洗净，沥干水分，去皮，切丝。
3. 热锅下油，煎香牛肉备用。
4. 再热锅下油，下胡萝卜丝、青瓜丝、本菇、大豆芽、韩国泡菜和调味料拌匀，盛起。
5. 白饭放入石头锅，饭面铺上炒好的牛肉和其他材料。
6. 将石头锅直接放在炉上加热，直至有啪啪声不断传出，以及有少许饭焦的气味即可熄火，加上鸡蛋黄即可。

其他 / Other

美食达人心动试味 / Gourmet's Comments

煮薯仔时要留意是否已软腍。
Be aware to cook potato until tender.

Baked portuguese chicken rice
葡国鸡焗饭

⏱ 50 分钟 / Minutes 👥 3 人 / Persons

Tips

不喜欢辣可不爆香咖喱，直接加入便可。
If you dislike spicy flavour, do not sauté curry and add direct.

材料	光鸡1/2只（约900克）/ 鸡蛋1只 / 薯仔（马铃薯）1个 / 洋葱1个 / 红葱头1粒 / 白饭4碗 / 咖喱粉1茶匙 / 咖喱酱1茶匙 / 粗盐少许
腌料	生粉1茶匙 / 盐1/2茶匙 / 生抽1/2茶匙 / 糖1/4茶匙
调味料	生抽1/2茶匙 / 盐1/4茶匙
汁料	椰汁100毫升 / 淡奶50毫升

Ingredients	1/2pc (about 900g) chicken / 1pc egg / 1pc potato / 1pc onion / 1pc shallot / 4 bowls of white rice / 1tsp curry powder / 1tsp curry paste / Little coarse salt.
Marinade	1tsp caltrop starch / 1/2tsp salt / 1/2tsp light soy sauce / 1/4tsp sugar
Seasonings	1/2tsp light soy sauce / 1/4tsp salt
Sauce	100ml coconut milk / 50ml evaporated milk

做法 Method

1. Rub chicken with coarse salt, wash, drain, cut into wedges, and marinate for 30 minutes. Whisk egg in a large bowl.

2. Shave potato, wash and cut into wedges. Peel onion, wash and cut into large wedges.

3. Heat wok with oil. Sauté onion and stir in a little salt.

4. Heat wok with oil again. Add in white rice, shallow-fry, stir in whisked egg. Set aside.

5. Heat wok with oil again. Sauté shallot, curry powder and curry paste, add in chicken and potato, stir in seasonings and some water. Cover and cook for 20 minutes. Add in onion, cook for 10 minutes until all ingredients are tender, stir in sauce and spread onto rice.

6. Bake in preheated oven at 190°C for 10 minutes until golden brown.

1. 光鸡用粗盐略擦，洗净，沥干水分，切块，加入腌料腌30分钟。鸡蛋放入大碗中打成蛋液。

2. 薯仔去皮，洗净，切块。洋葱去衣，洗净，切大块。

3. 热锅下油，加入洋葱略炒，下少许盐调味。

4. 再热锅下油，加入白饭拌炒，加入蛋液炒匀，放入深碟备用。

5. 再热锅下油，爆香红葱头、咖喱粉和咖喱酱，加入鸡块和薯仔拌匀，下调味料和适量水，盖好锅盖，煮20分钟。再加入洋葱煮约10分钟至各材料已软腍，加入汁料淋在饭面。

6. 放到已预热的焗炉内，以190℃焗约10分钟至金黄色即成。

其他 / Other

美食达人心动试味 / Gourmet's Comments

煮好的饭要焖透才盛起。
After cooked, cover rice for a while before use.

Tomato pot with assorted mushrooms rice
番茄盅杂菌饭

⏱ 25 分钟 / Minutes   👥 2 人 / Persons

Tips

不用番茄可改用三色椒,效果相似但味道不同。
Tomatoes can be replaced by green, yellow and red sweet peppers, effect is similar but different taste.

材料 番茄1~2个 / 杂色饭（红米饭、白米饭、糙米饭）1/2碗
鲜杂菌50克 / 松子仁1~2汤匙
烟肉2片 / 薄荷1~2片（装饰）

调味料 盐1/2茶匙 / 糖1/2茶匙 / 日式烧汁1汤匙

Ingredients: 1-2pcs tomato / 1/2 bowl of colorful rice(red rice, white rice, brown rice) / 50g assorted fresh mushrooms / 1-2tbsps pine nuts 2slices bacon / 1-2pcs mint (for dressing)

Seasonings: 1/2tsp salt / 1/2tsp sugar / 1tbsp Japanese sauce

做法 Method

1. Mince the bacon, toast the pine nuts. Blanch and rinse the assorted mushrooms thoroughly, and diced.

2. Fry the bacon in a heated wok until fragrant, add the diced assorted mushrooms, colorful rice and pine nuts, stir-fry well, add seasonings and mix well.

3. Scoop out the tomatoes, put the fried rice into it.

4. Preheat the oven for 2-3 minutes, put the tomatoes into the oven for 10 minutes, then ready to serve.

1. 烟肉切碎，松子仁烘香。杂菌飞水后过冷，切碎。

2. 热锅炒香烟肉，加入杂菌粒、杂色饭和松子仁炒匀，加入调味料拌匀。

3. 番茄挖空，放入炒饭。

4. 焗炉预热2~3分钟，放入番茄盅焗10分钟，即成。

Other 其他

美食达人心动试味 / Gourmet's Comments

每个迷你糯米鸡都要大小均匀，材料的分量要一致。
Each mini steamed glutinous rice with chicken should be wrapped equally and in similar size.

Mini steamed glutinous rice with chicken
迷你糯米鸡

40 分钟 / Minutes
6 人 / Persons

Tips

蒸糯米时不用加水，因糯米在浸水时已吸收了水分。
It is unnecessary to add water when steaming glutinous rice as it absorbs enough water during soaking.

材料	鸡肉1块 / 叉烧60克 / 冬菇2只 / 糯米400克 / 荷叶2块 / 生抽少许
鸡肉腌料	生粉1/2茶匙 / 盐1/4茶匙 / 胡椒粉1/4茶匙
调味料	蚝油1汤匙 / 水120毫升
糯米调味料	鸡粉1茶匙 / 盐1/2茶匙 / 麻油1/2茶匙 / 糖1/4茶匙
芡汁	生粉1茶匙 / 水2汤匙

Ingredients	1pc chicken meat / 60g roasted pork / 2pcs black mushroom / 400g glutinous rice / 2pcs lotus leaf / Little light soy sauce
Marinade of chicken	1/2tsp caltrop starch / 1/4tsp salt / 1/4tsp pepper
Seasonings	1tbsp oyster sauce / 120ml water
Seasoning of glutinous rice	1tsp chicken powder / 1/2tsp salt / 1/2tsp sesame oil / 1/4tsp sugar
Thickening	1tsp caltrop starch / 2tbsps water

做法 / Method

1. Wash glutinous rice, and soak for 3 hours, drain. Stir in seasoning of glutinous rice. Put into steamer, steam over water for 20 minutes, and flip it over in the steamer 2-3 times.

2. Soak lotus leaves in hot water, pat dry, and cut into 8 portions.

3. Wash chicken meat, dice and marinate.

4. Soak black mushrooms, remove stem, dice and add in a little light soy sauce.

5. Heat wok with oil. Stir-fry chicken and black mushrooms, add in roasted pork and seasonings, stir in thickening, dish up, and divide into 8 portions.

6. Place a piece of lotus leaf on table, add in some glutinous rice, put a portion of ingredients on top, then glutinous rice, and wrap with lotus leaf to form square. Place opening downwards, arrange on steamer, and steam over water for 8-10 minutes.

1. 糯米淘洗净，用水浸3小时，沥干水分。加入糯米调味料拌匀，放入蒸笼，以大火隔水蒸20分钟，期间翻动糯米饭2~3次。

2. 荷叶用沸水浸泡后，抹干水分，剪裁成8份。

3. 鸡肉洗净，切粒，加鸡肉腌料拌匀。

4. 冬菇浸软，去蒂，切粒，加少许生抽调味。

5. 热锅下油，将鸡肉和冬菇炒熟，加入叉烧和调味料拌匀，下芡汁炒匀，盛起，分成8份。

6. 先将一块荷叶放台面，铺上一层糯米，放入一份材料，再盖上一层糯米，将荷叶包紧呈方形，封口向下，排放在蒸笼上，隔水蒸8~10分钟即可。

其他 / Other

美食达人心动试味 / *Gourmet's Comments*

鱼露味道虽然很香，但不要下太多，否则会夺去烧鸭的香味。

Although fish sauce is fragrant, do not add too much. Otherwise, it will override the aroma of roasted duck.

Rice with roasted duck in soup
烧鸭泡饭

⏱ 15 分钟 / Minutes   👥 2 人 / Persons

Tips

烧鸭可改用烧鹅或鸡，菜可改用任何菜。

You may use roasted goose or chicken to substitute roasted duck, and use any other kinds of vegetables to substitute Choi Sum.

材料　　烧鸭1/4 只 / 菜心4 条 / 白饭2 碗 / 葱2棵
调味料　鱼露1 茶匙 / 鸡粉1/2 茶匙 / 老抽1/4 茶匙

Ingredients 1/4pc roasted duck / 4pcs Choi Sum / 2 bowls of white rice / 2pcs spring onion
Seasonings   1tsp fish sauce / 1/2tsp chicken powder / 1/4tsp dark soy sauce

做法 Method

1. Chop roasted duck.
2. Wash spring onion, remove root and end part, and dice.
3. Wash Choi Sum, and remove old leaf.
4. Boil 4 bowls of water in wok. Add in roasted duck and seasonings, and cook for a while. Add in Choi Sum, and cook until it become the roasted duck soup.
5. Keep white rice warm, put into a large bowl, add in roasted duck soup, sprinkle diced spring onion and serve.

1. 烧鸭切块。
2. 葱洗净，切去根部和尾部，切成葱花。
3. 菜心洗净，摘去老叶。
4. 在锅中煮滚4碗水，加入烧鸭和调味料，煮片刻，放下菜心再煮滚，熄火，即成烧鸭汤。
5. 白饭保温，放入大碗内，倒入烧鸭汤，撒上葱花即成。

其他 / Other

美食达人心动试味 / Gourmet's Comments

倒入饭后不要煮,即可盛起。
Do not cook after pouring into rice, and serve.

Rice with mixed white gourd in soup
杂锦冬瓜粒泡饭

20 分钟 / Minutes　　3 人 / Persons

Tips

冬瓜不要切得太碎,否则煮脸后会变成蓉。
Do not cut white gourd into tiny pieces. Otherwise, it will become puree after cooking.

材料	冬瓜300克 / 猪瘦肉100克 / 冬菇3只 / 白饭3碗 / 上汤2杯
腌料	生粉1茶匙 / 盐1/4茶匙 / 糖1/4茶匙 / 胡椒粉1/4茶匙
调味料	盐1/2茶匙 / 鸡粉1/2茶匙 / 胡椒粉1/4茶匙

Ingredients	300g white gourd / 100g lean pork / 3pcs black mushroom / 3bowls of white rice / 2cups of broth
Marinade	1tsp caltrop starch / 1/4tsp salt / 1/4tsp sugar / 1/4tsp pepper
Seasonings	1/2tsp salt / 1/2tsp chicken powder / 1/4tsp pepper

做法 Method

1. Shave white gourd, remove seed, wash and dice.
2. Wash lean pork, dice and marinate.
3. Soak black mushrooms, remove stem and dice.
4. Keep rice warm and put into a large bowl.
5. Heat wok with oil. Stir-fry diced black mushrooms and diced white gourd, add in diced lean pork and cook until well done. Add in broth and cook for a while, stir in seasonings, pour into rice to make rice in soup.

1. 冬瓜去皮去籽，洗净切粒。
2. 猪瘦肉洗净，切粒，加入腌料拌匀。
3. 冬菇浸软，去蒂，切粒。
4. 白饭保温，放入大碗内。
5. 热锅下油，下冬菇粒和冬瓜粒略炒，加入瘦肉粒炒至熟，注入上汤待滚片刻，加入调味料，倒入饭内即成泡饭。

其他 / Other

美食达人心动试味 / Gourmet's Comments

芒果和黑、白糯米的配搭，色彩丰富，加上椰香十足的汁料，更是色香味俱全。

Black and white glutinous rice match up with mangoes and sauce, colorful and tasteful.

Glutinous rice with mangoes
香芒糯米饭

20 分钟 / Minutes　　3 人 / Persons

Tips

黑糯米较硬，浸泡时间应较白糯米长，否则蒸出来的饭会软硬不一。

Black glutinous rice is harder than white glutinous rice, so it should be soak for longer. Otherwise, texture of steamed rice will be mixed.

材料	糯米200克 / 黑糯米50克 / 椰汁1/2杯 / 芒果2~3个 / 班兰叶（香兰叶）1~2片
汁料	椰汁1/3杯 / 盐1/2茶匙 / 木薯粉1茶匙 / 水3茶匙 / 班兰叶（香兰叶）1片 (切段)

Ingredients	200g glutinous rice / 50g black glutinous rice / 1/2 cup of coconut milk / 2-3pcs mango / 1-2pcs pandan leaf
Sauce	1/3 cup of coconut milk / 1/2tsp salt / 1tsp potato powder / 3tsp water / 1pc pandan leaf(cut segment)

做法 / Method

1. Wash and soak the white and black glutinous rice in water for 1-2 hours respectively, then drain.
2. Mix the rice, put the rice on a pandan leaf, move the whole thing into a steamer lined with a white cheese cloth, steam it over high heat for 10-15 minutes. Flip it over twice during cooking, sprinkle it with some coconut milk and mix them well.
3. Skin and stone the mangoes. Set aside.
4. Cook the sauce in a pot until the liquid thickens.
5. Make some rice cakes with the glutinous rice and serve them with mangoes and sauce.

1. 黑糯米及糯米分别浸1~2小时。然后淘洗干净，沥干。
2. 黑、白糯米拌匀，放于班兰叶上，再放在已垫白洋布的蒸笼以大火蒸10~15分钟，期间翻动糯米饭2次，并洒点椰汁拌匀。
3. 芒果去皮和去核，备用。
4. 汁料置煲中煮至浓稠。
5. 把糯米饭做成饭团伴以去皮芒果和汁料享用。

其他 / Other

美食达人心动试味 / Gourmet's Comments

包入馅料时不要包得太多，否则会令馅料溢出。
Do not wrap too much filling. Otherwise, it will spill out.

Chinese glutinous rice roll
粢饭

1 小时 / Hours
3 人 / Persons

Tips

如想改为甜食，馅料可用油条和糖。
If sweet flavour is preferred, you may use deep-fried twisted dough stick (deep-fried noodles) and sugar as filling.

材料	糯米 300 克 / 水 1½ 杯 / 上汤（浸过米的分量）
馅料	榨菜 1/2 个 / 虾米 30 克 / 猪肉松 35 克

Ingredients	300g glutinous rice / 1½ cups of water / broth (the amount should be enough to soak rice)
Fillings	1/2pc preserved vegetables / 30g dried shrimps / 35g pork floss

做法 / Method

1. Wash glutinous rice, add in broth and water, soak for 3 hours. Drain water, steam in wok over water for 30 minutes until well done. Flip it over in the wok continuously.

2. Wash preserved vegetables, soak in water to reduce salty flavour, dice.

3. Wash dried shrimps, soak and dice.

4. Heat wok with oil. Sauté preserved vegetables and dried shrimps. Set aside.

5. Place a piece of wet cloth on table, then put plastic wrap, glutinous rice, fillings on top, and roll into rice dumpling. Tight two ends and serve.

---

1. 糯米淘洗净，注入上汤和水浸约 3 小时，隔去水分，放入锅中隔水蒸约 30 分钟至熟，要不时翻动。

2. 榨菜洗净，用水略浸，减去咸味，切碎。

3. 虾米洗净，浸透，切碎。

4. 热锅下油，爆香榨菜和虾米，盛起备用。

5. 放一块湿布在台上，铺上保鲜纸，放上糯米饭铺平，放入馅料，卷实成饭团，两头扎紧即成。

Other 其他

美食达人心动试味 | Gourmet's Comments

锅巴吸满芡汁,配上杂菌又香又脆。
Crispy rice and mushrooms are good match.

Crispy rice with assorted mushrooms
杂菌锅巴

15 分钟 / Minutes
6 人 / Persons

材料 锅巴1包／本菇（本占地菇）1包／金菇（金针菇）1包／西兰花1棵／蒜蓉2茶匙／姜蓉1茶匙／酒少许

芡汁 蚝油3汤匙／老抽1茶匙／上汤1/3杯／生粉2茶匙／糖1茶匙／盐1/4茶匙

Ingredients 1 packet of crispy rice / 1 packet of shimeji mushrooms / 1 packet of golden mushrooms / 1 head of broccoli / 2tsps garlic puree / 1tsp ginger puree / Some wine

Thickening 3tbsps oyster sauce / 1tsp dark soy sauce / 1/3cup of broth / 2tsps caltrop starch / 1tsp sugar / 1/4tsp salt

做法 Method

1. Remove the stem of the mushrooms, wash slightly and then set aside.

2. Remove the rough skin of the broccoli, wash thoroughly, blanch, rinse and then set aside.

3. Put 1-2 tbsps of oil in a heated frying pan, sauté garlic puree and ginger puree. Add in broccoli, stir-fry for a while, splash in some wine, sprinkle 1-2 tbsps of broth and then set aside.

4. Pour the thickening into the frying pan and bring it to a boil. Add the mushrooms, cook until softened and then set aside.

5. Put the assorted mushrooms and broccoli on the same plate to be served with crispy rice.

1. 把本菇和金针菇去蒂，稍冲水备用。

2. 西兰花去掉硬皮，洗净，飞水，过冷，备用。

3. 热锅下油1~2汤匙，爆香蒜蓉和姜蓉，放入西兰花兜炒片刻，溅酒，洒1~2汤匙上汤，盛起。

4. 将芡汁倒入锅中煮滚，放入本菇和金菇煮软，盛起。

5. 杂菌与西兰花同上碟，伴以锅巴享用。

烹饪小词典
Cooking key words

做菜和味道的常用语
Common phrases of cooking and tastes

普通话 Mandarrin	英文 English	广东话 Cantonese （拼音）
食物味道 Taste		
熟	cooked	熟 sug
没熟	raw	未熟 mei sug
生 / 没熟	uncooked	生（未熟）seng
太咸	too salty	太咸 tai ham
太长时间	too long	太耐 tai noi
不够咸	not salty enough	唔够咸 m geo ham
不够甜	not sweet enough	唔够甜 m geo tim
香	aromatic	香 heng
臭	stink	臭 ceo
甜	sweet	甜 tim
酸	sour	酸 xun
苦	bitter	苦 fu
辣	spicy	辣 lad
咸	salty	咸 ham
煮菜方式 Cooking Method		
切片	slice	切片 qid pin
切长一点	cut longer	切长少少 qid ceng xiu-xiu
切短一点	cut shorter	切短少少 qid tün xiu-xiu
切块	cut into wedges	切块 qid fai
切粒	cut into dice	切粒粒 qid neb-neb
蒸	steam	蒸 jing
炸	deep-fry	炸 za
煎	shallow-fry	煎 jin
炒菜	stir-fry vegetables	炒菜 cau coi
焯菜	blanch vegetables	渌菜 lug coi
煲汤	cook soup	煲汤 bou tong
炆猪肉	stew pork	炆猪肉 men ju yug

常用调味品（附广东话发音）
Common seasonings

granulated sugar
砂糖 sa tong

brown sugar
黄糖 wong tong

slab sugar
片糖 pin tong

rock sugar
冰糖 bing tong

salt
盐 yim

corn oil
粟米油 sug mei yeo

olive oil
橄榄油 gem lam yeo

cooking oil
生油 seng yeo

butter
牛油 ngeo yeo

sesame oil 麻油 ma yeo	light soy sauce 生抽 seng chau	dark soy sauce 老抽 lou chau
oyster sauce 蚝油 hou yeo	fish sauce 鱼露 yu lou	ketchup 番茄酱 fan ke zeng
vinegar 醋 cou	wine 酒 zeo	cornstarch 鹰粟粉 ying sug fen

caltrop starch 生粉 seng fen	**flour** 面粉 min fen	**MSG** 味精 mei jing
chili bean sauce 豆瓣酱 deo ban zeng	**satay sauce** 沙爹酱 sa de zeng	 **miso** 面酱 min zeng
 **fermented black beans** 豆豉 deo xi	 **red beancurd** 南乳 nam yu	 **fermented beancurd** 腐乳 fu yu

black pepper sauce
黑椒烧汁 hak jiu xiu zeb

Tabasco
辣椒汁 lad jiu zeb

curry powder
咖喱粉 ga lei fen

chicken powder
鸡粉 gei fen

chicken broth
鸡汤 gei tong

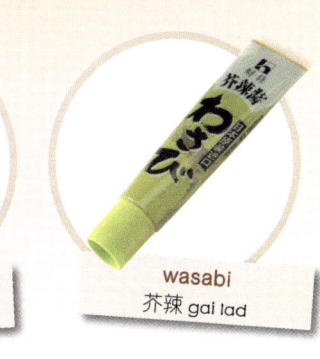

wasabi
芥辣 gai lad

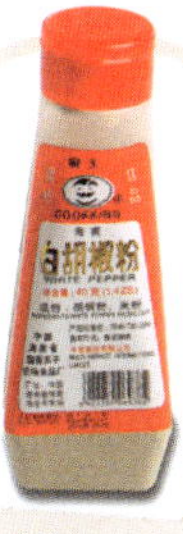

pepper
胡椒粉 wu jiu fen

spices
香料 heng liu

honey
蜜糖 med tong

常用技巧
Common skills

切角 Cut into triangles	把物料移动，切成三角形。 Roll the ingredients and cut into triangles.
骨牌 Domino	物料先切成长形，再修切成长方形。 Cut the ingredients into long pieces, and then rectangles.
去衣 Peel off the thin layer	把栗子放热水中煮1~2分钟，去掉栗子外皮。 Cook chestnuts into boiling water for 1-2 minutes, peel off the thin layer of chestnuts.
去皮 Shave	用刨子削去物料外皮。 Shave off the skin of the ingredients.
幼切粗剁 Shred and chop	将肉切成薄片再切条，再切粒才剁，就可不用剁太久。 Slice meat and shred, dice and chop to minimize chopping time.
料头 Side ingredients	泛指姜、葱、蒜、红葱头或辣椒，协助提升物料的香味。 Usually refer to ginger, spring onion, garlic, shallot and chili which make ingredients more aromatic.
免治 Mince	将肉剁碎。 Chop to make minced meat.
蓉 Puree	剁至最幼细。 Chop until become puree.
泡油 Blanch with oil	将物料放入八成滚油中2~3分钟，取出沥油。 Cook ingredients in 80% boiled oil for 2-3 minutes, take out and drain.
飞水（汆水） Blanch	物料放入滚水中焯2~3分钟，取出过冷。 Cook ingredients in boiling water for 2-3 minutes, take out and rinse with cold water.
过冷 Rinse	飞水后，将食物用冷水或冰水略冲洗一下，再炒煮时令食物较爽口。 Wash ingredients in cool water after blanch, to make it taste better.
白镬（锅） Wok without adding oil	没有添加任何物料、酱料或油等，只是把镬（锅）烧热后直接下物料烘干水分。 Without any ingredients, sauce or oil, dry the ingredients in a heated wok directly.
爆香 Sauté	用少量油加热，放入料头略煎至出味的程序。 Slightly shallow-fry side ingredients till aromatic with some heated oil.